# Azerbaijan

## Introduction to the Azerbaijan Travel Guide

Welcome to the enchanting world of Azerbaijan, a country that seamlessly blends rich history, captivating culture, stunning landscapes, and modern allure. Nestled at the crossroads of Eastern Europe and Western Asia, Azerbaijan offers travelers a tapestry of experiences that range from exploring ancient archaeological sites to indulging in sumptuous cuisine, from lounging on picturesque Caspian Sea beaches to immersing yourself in vibrant city life.

This travel guide is your passport to discovering the diverse and fascinating facets of Azerbaijan. Whether you're an intrepid adventurer, a history enthusiast, a culinary connoisseur, or simply seeking a unique and memorable vacation, Azerbaijan has something extraordinary to offer. Join us on a journey through the country's vibrant cities, tranquil towns, and breathtaking natural wonders as we uncover the best attractions, foods, accommodations, and activities that this remarkable destination has to offer.

Let's embark on an unforgettable journey through the Land of Fire, where ancient traditions meet modern marvels, and where the warm hospitality of the Azerbaijani people awaits you.

## Table of Contents

## Introduction

Geography and Location

History and Culture

Visa Requirements

## Getting There and Around

Airports

Public Transportation

Driving in Azerbaijan

## Top Destinations

Baku

Sheki

Gabala

Ganja

Gobustan National Park

## Things to Do

Explore Baku's Old City

Visit Historical Sites

Discover Natural Wonders

Enjoy Azerbaijani Cuisine

Attend Festivals

## Travel Tips

Language and Communication

Currency and Money

Safety and Health

Etiquette and Culture

## 1. Introduction

### Geography and Location

Azerbaijan is located in the South Caucasus region, bordering the Caspian Sea to the east. It shares borders with Russia to the north, Georgia to the northwest, Armenia to the west, and Iran to the south. The country's diverse geography includes mountains, plains, and a beautiful coastline along the Caspian Sea.

### History and Culture

Azerbaijan has a rich cultural heritage, influenced by Persian, Turkish, and Russian civilizations. The capital city, Baku, is known for its blend of modern architecture and historic old town. The country is also famous for its music, particularly mugham (traditional Azerbaijani music) and its role in the development of jazz.

### Visa Requirements

Before traveling to Azerbaijan, check the visa requirements for your nationality. Many travelers can obtain a visa on arrival, while others may need to apply in advance. Make sure your passport is valid for at least six months beyond your intended departure date.

## 2. Getting There and Around

## Airports

The main international gateway to Azerbaijan is Heydar Aliyev International Airport in Baku. There are also airports in other major cities like Ganja and Nakhchivan, which offer domestic and limited international flights. To reach more remote destinations, you may need to use domestic flights or ground transportation.

## Public Transportation

Azerbaijan has a well-developed public transportation system, including buses, trams, and metro systems in cities like Baku and Ganja. Intercity buses and trains are also available for traveling between cities. Taxis and ride-sharing apps like Uber are common for getting around locally.

## Driving in Azerbaijan

If you plan to rent a car, be aware that traffic can be chaotic in some areas, and road signs may be in Azerbaijani. An international driving permit and insurance are recommended. Make sure to obey traffic laws and drive safely.

# 3. Top Destinations

## Baku

Baku, the capital, is a bustling metropolis known for its modern skyscrapers, historic Old City (Icherisheher), and the Flame Towers. Don't miss attractions like the Maiden Tower, Palace of the Shirvanshahs, and the Heydar Aliyev Center, an architectural marvel.

## Sheki

Sheki is a charming city nestled in the mountains, famous for its exquisite Sheki Khan's Palace, built in the 18th century. Explore the city's cobblestone streets, visit local markets, and enjoy the scenic beauty of the region.

## Gabala

Gabala is a popular resort town surrounded by lush forests and the Tufandag Mountain. Outdoor enthusiasts can enjoy activities like hiking, skiing (in winter), and zip-lining. Gabala also offers cultural attractions and a relaxed atmosphere.

## Ganja

Ganja is Azerbaijan's second-largest city and known for its history, parks, and vibrant atmosphere. Explore Nizami Street, visit the Nizami Mausoleum, and enjoy the city's green spaces, like Khan Baghi Park.

### Gobustan National Park

Gobustan is a UNESCO World Heritage Site renowned for its ancient rock petroglyphs, mud volcanoes, and unique geological formations. Take a guided tour to learn about the region's history and geological wonders.

## 4. Things to Do

### Explore Baku's Old City

Wander through the narrow streets of Icherisheher, where you'll find historic buildings, museums, shops, and restaurants. Be sure to visit the Maiden Tower and the Palace of the Shirvanshahs.

### Visit Historical Sites

Explore the ancient city of Shamakhi, the cave city of Ateshgah, and the mysterious Yanar Dag, where natural gas has been burning for centuries. These sites offer a glimpse into Azerbaijan's rich history and culture.

### Discover Natural Wonders

Hike in the Caucasus Mountains, take a dip in the Caspian Sea, or visit the Gaval Dash, a musical rock that produces melodic sounds when struck. Azerbaijan's diverse landscapes are waiting to be explored.

### Enjoy Azerbaijani Cuisine

Indulge in local delicacies like kebabs, plov (rice pilaf), dolma (stuffed grape leaves), and baklava. Try Azerbaijani tea and visit local markets to taste fresh produce and spices.

### Attend Festivals

Check the calendar for festivals and events happening during your visit. Novruz Bayram, celebrated in March, is one of the most important cultural events, marked by vibrant traditions and festivities.

## 5. Travel Tips

### Language and Communication

Azerbaijani is the official language, but many people in urban areas speak English and Russian. Learning a few basic Azerbaijani phrases can enhance your travel experience.

Currency and Money

The currency is the Azerbaijani Manat (AZN). Credit cards are widely accepted in major cities, but it's advisable to carry some cash for smaller establishments and rural areas.

Safety and Health

Azerbaijan is generally safe for travelers. Ensure your vaccinations are up-to-date and have travel insurance. Tap water is not recommended for drinking; opt for bottled water.

Etiquette and Culture

Respect local customs and traditions. Dress modestly when visiting religious sites, and ask for permission before taking photos of people. It's customary to remove your shoes when entering someone's home.

Enjoy your journey through Azerbaijan, a land of captivating landscapes, rich history, and warm hospitality. Explore the diverse regions, savor the flavors of Azerbaijani cuisine, and immerse yourself in the unique culture of this remarkable country. Safe travels!

what can i see in Baku

Baku, the capital of Azerbaijan, is a vibrant and modern city with a rich history and a wealth of attractions to explore. Here are some of the top things to see and do in Baku:

Old City (Icherisheher): The historic core of Baku is a UNESCO World Heritage Site and a must-visit. Explore the narrow winding streets, visit the Maiden Tower (Giz Galasi), and discover ancient mosques, caravanserais, and palaces.

Flame Towers: These iconic skyscrapers dominate the city's skyline. At night, they are illuminated with a mesmerizing display of flames and lights. It's a sight you won't want to miss.

Heydar Aliyev Center: Designed by renowned architect Zaha Hadid, this futuristic building is an architectural masterpiece. Even if you don't go inside, the exterior is a work of art worth admiring.

Palace of the Shirvanshahs: This medieval palace complex is another UNESCO World Heritage Site. Explore the beautifully preserved palace, mosques, bathhouses, and mausoleums, all set against the backdrop of the Old City.

Maiden Tower: Climb to the top of this ancient tower for panoramic views of Baku and the Caspian Sea. Inside, you'll find a museum showcasing the tower's history.

Baku Boulevard: Stroll along the promenade lining the Caspian Sea. The boulevard offers beautiful views, cafes, and recreational activities like bike rentals.

Nizami Street: Baku's main shopping and entertainment street is lined with shops, boutiques, restaurants, and cafes. It's a great place for a leisurely walk and some retail therapy.

Carpet Museum: Azerbaijan is famous for its carpets, and this museum displays a stunning collection of traditional Azerbaijani carpets and rugs. The building itself is shaped like a rolled-up carpet.

Ganjlik Mall: If you're in the mood for shopping, this mall offers a wide range of stores and a modern cinema complex.

Fountain Square: This lively square is the heart of Baku's entertainment and nightlife. It's a great place to enjoy street performances, cafes, and people-watching.

Taza Pir Mosque: One of Baku's largest mosques, Taza Pir is an impressive architectural sight with its turquoise domes and minarets.

National Museum of Azerbaijan History: Explore the country's history, culture, and archaeology through an extensive collection of artifacts and exhibits.

Azerbaijan Carpet Museum: If you're interested in learning more about the art of Azerbaijani carpet weaving, this museum provides an in-depth look at this cultural tradition.

Boulevard Park: This lush park stretches along the Caspian Sea and offers green spaces, sculptures, and a great place to relax.

Bibi-Heybat Mosque: Located on a hill overlooking the city, this mosque is not only architecturally stunning but also holds religious significance for Azerbaijanis.

Gara Garayev Cultural Center: An impressive architectural complex with cultural and artistic exhibitions, including the Gara Garayev Museum.

These are just a few of the many attractions you can explore in Baku. The city's unique blend of modernity and history makes it a captivating destination for travelers.

what are the best foods from Baku

Baku, the capital of Azerbaijan, offers a delightful culinary experience with a mix of traditional Azerbaijani and international cuisine. Here are some of the best foods to try while in Baku:

Plov (Pilaf): Azerbaijani plov is a delicious rice dish cooked with saffron, lamb, and a variety of spices. It's often garnished with fried onions, dried fruits, and chestnuts.

Dolma: Dolma consists of grape leaves or vegetables stuffed with a mixture of ground meat, rice, and herbs. It's typically served with yogurt or a garlic sauce.

Kebabs: Azerbaijani kebabs are famous for their flavor. Try lamb, beef, or chicken kebabs, which are often marinated with spices and grilled to perfection.

Dushbara: These small dumplings are usually filled with minced meat and served in a flavorful broth. They are a favorite comfort food in Azerbaijan.

Lavangi: Lavangi is a unique Azerbaijani dish made with stuffed chicken or fish. It's typically filled with walnuts, onions, and aromatic spices.

Badimjan Dolmasi: This dish features stuffed eggplants with a tasty mixture of ground meat, onions, and herbs, all simmered in a savory tomato sauce.

Kutab: Kutab is a popular Azerbaijani snack or appetizer. It's a thin, pancake-like pastry filled with minced meat, herbs, or cheese.

Shah Pilaf: A special version of plov, Shah Pilaf includes nuts, dried fruits, and saffron, giving it a rich and luxurious flavor.

Dovga: This yogurt soup is a traditional Azerbaijani dish made with yogurt, herbs, and sometimes rice. It's often consumed during hot summer months for its refreshing qualities.

Azerbaijani Sweets: Indulge in sweets like pakhlava (baklava), shakarbura (sweet pastries), and shekerbura (filled cookies) with a cup of Azerbaijani tea.

Lavash: Azerbaijani flatbread, known as lavash, is a staple and often served alongside meals. It's thin, soft, and perfect for wrapping kebabs or enjoying with cheese and herbs.

Azerbaijani Tea: Azerbaijani tea culture is a significant part of the culinary experience. Tea is typically served in small, glass cups, often accompanied by jam or pastries.

Dushbere Soup: A hearty and flavorful soup made with small dumplings, dushbere is a popular choice for those looking to warm up on a cool day.

Azeri-style Pizza (Pide): Azerbaijani pide is similar to Turkish pide. It's a boat-shaped, thin crust pizza typically topped with minced meat, vegetables, and herbs.

Saffron Ice Cream: Cool off with saffron-infused ice cream, a refreshing treat with a unique flavor.

When dining in Baku, don't forget to try local restaurants and street vendors to experience the full range of Azerbaijani cuisine. The combination of savory meats, aromatic herbs, and sweet treats will leave your taste buds satisfied and your culinary curiosity fulfilled.

what are the best restaurants in Baku

Baku offers a wide range of dining options, from traditional Azerbaijani cuisine to international flavors. Here are some of the best restaurants in Baku, known for their quality food and ambiance:

Nar - This restaurant chain is known for its modern Azerbaijani cuisine and a beautiful view of the Caspian Sea. The menu features a variety of traditional dishes prepared with a contemporary twist.

Dolmama - A popular spot in the heart of Baku, Dolmama serves traditional Azerbaijani dishes, including a delicious selection of dolma and plov. The atmosphere is warm and inviting.

Mangal Steakhouse - As the name suggests, Mangal Steakhouse is a top choice for meat lovers. They offer a variety of perfectly grilled steaks and other meat dishes.

Art Club Restaurant - This trendy restaurant combines art and cuisine, offering a menu that includes both Azerbaijani and European dishes. The decor is stylish and often features art exhibitions.

Sirvansah Restaurant - Located in Baku's Old City, Sirvansah provides an authentic Azerbaijani dining experience with live music, traditional Azerbaijani dishes, and a charming ambiance.

Firuze Restaurant - Firuze offers a fusion of Azerbaijani and Middle Eastern cuisine. It's known for its kebabs and beautiful interior design.

Mugham Club - Enjoy traditional Azerbaijani music and dance performances while savoring local dishes at Mugham Club. It's a great place to immerse yourself in Azerbaijani culture.

Xalca Restaurant - Located in the Old City, Xalca Restaurant is renowned for its cozy atmosphere and a menu that includes a variety of traditional Azerbaijani dishes.

Art Garden - This restaurant is known for its picturesque garden setting and a menu featuring Azerbaijani and European cuisine. It's an excellent choice for a romantic dinner.

Sehrli Tandir - Sehrli Tandir specializes in Azerbaijani tandoori dishes, including succulent lamb cooked in a clay oven. The restaurant's decor reflects traditional Azerbaijani culture.

Dəhliz - Dəhliz offers a mix of Azerbaijani and Turkish cuisine. The rooftop terrace provides a great view of Baku and the Caspian Sea.

Baku Fish House - Seafood lovers should visit Baku Fish House for its excellent selection of fresh fish and seafood dishes prepared with Azerbaijani and Mediterranean flavors.

Museum Inn - This restaurant, located in the Old City, has a unique atmosphere with its museum-like decor. They serve Azerbaijani and international dishes.

Shah - Shah is known for its upscale dining experience and exquisite Azerbaijani and Middle Eastern cuisine. The elegant interior and attentive service make it a top choice for special occasions.

Zeytun Restaurant - A family-friendly restaurant offering a variety of Azerbaijani and international dishes. It's known for its pleasant garden seating.

These are just a few of the many dining options available in Baku. Whether you're in the mood for traditional Azerbaijani cuisine or international flavors, Baku's culinary scene has something for everyone. Be sure to make reservations, especially for popular restaurants, to ensure you secure a table.

what are some lesser known travel spots in Baku

While Baku has its share of well-known attractions, there are also some lesser-known travel spots and hidden gems that offer unique experiences and a break from the crowds. Here are a few to consider:

Mardakan Castle: Located just outside of Baku, Mardakan Castle is a historical gem that often gets overlooked. It's a well-preserved medieval fortress with impressive architecture and beautiful views of the surrounding countryside.

Yanar Dag: This natural wonder is a hillside that continuously burns due to the presence of natural gas. It's often referred to as the "Burning Mountain" and is located about 25 kilometers from Baku. Witnessing the flames at night is particularly mesmerizing.

Gala Open Air Museum: Situated in a small village near Baku, Gala Open Air Museum offers a glimpse into Azerbaijani rural life. It features traditional Azerbaijani houses, artifacts, and exhibits that showcase the country's rich cultural heritage.

Ateshgah Fire Temple: Located in Surakhani, a suburb of Baku, this unique temple complex was once a place of worship for Zoroastrians. It features a central temple with a natural gas-fueled eternal flame.

Bibi-Heybat Mosque: This beautiful mosque is located on the outskirts of Baku and offers breathtaking views of the city and the Caspian Sea. The mosque itself is an architectural marvel with its turquoise domes and minarets.

The House Museum of Mir Jalal Pashayev: This museum is dedicated to the Azerbaijani writer Mir Jalal Pashayev. It's a charming house-museum filled with his personal belongings, manuscripts, and a peaceful garden.

Mountainous Shirvan National Park: For those interested in nature and hiking, this national park offers opportunities to explore the stunning landscapes and diverse flora and fauna of the region. It's a bit further from Baku but worth the journey.

Gobustan Rock Art Cultural Landscape: While not entirely unknown, Gobustan is often overshadowed by the nearby petroglyphs. Explore the lesser-visited areas of Gobustan to discover more ancient rock carvings and unique geological formations.

Baku Metro Stations: The Baku Metro is not just a means of transportation; it's a subterranean art gallery. Some of the metro stations are beautifully decorated with mosaics, sculptures, and intricate architectural designs. Don't miss stations like Nariman Narimanov and Khatai.

Boulevard Walk: While the Baku Boulevard is well-known, many visitors overlook some of its quieter and more secluded sections. Explore the less crowded areas for a tranquil stroll along the Caspian Sea.

These hidden gems and lesser-known spots in Baku provide a chance to delve deeper into Azerbaijani culture, history, and natural beauty away from the hustle and bustle of the city center. Don't hesitate to venture off the beaten path to discover these hidden treasures during your visit to Baku.

what activities must i experince in Baku

Baku offers a wide range of activities to make your visit memorable. Whether you're interested in history, culture, outdoor adventures, or simply enjoying the local atmosphere, there's something for everyone. Here are some must-experience activities in Baku:

Explore the Old City (Icherisheher): Wander through the narrow streets of Baku's historic core. Visit the Maiden Tower, Palace of the Shirvanshahs, and the many museums and shops within this UNESCO World Heritage Site.

Witness the Flame Towers: Marvel at the iconic Flame Towers, which come to life with a mesmerizing display of flames and lights at night.

Visit Heydar Aliyev Center: Explore the futuristic architecture and interior exhibits of this renowned cultural center designed by Zaha Hadid.

Enjoy a Baku Boulevard Stroll: Take a leisurely walk along the Baku Boulevard, a promenade by the Caspian Sea. You can rent bikes or simply enjoy the sea breeze and beautiful views.

Attend a Mugham Performance: Experience traditional Azerbaijani music by attending a mugham performance. These soulful and evocative musical events are held at venues like the Mugham Club.

Try Azerbaijani Cuisine: Sample the rich flavors of Azerbaijani cuisine. Don't miss dishes like plov, dolma, kebabs, and Azerbaijani sweets like pakhlava and shekerbura.

Take a Baku Night Tour: Baku comes alive at night with its illuminated buildings and waterfront. Consider a night tour to capture the city's magic after sunset.

Visit Modern Art Galleries: Explore Baku's contemporary art scene by visiting galleries like the YARAT Contemporary Art Space and Baku Museum of Modern Art.

Discover Gobustan Petroglyphs: Explore Gobustan National Park to see ancient rock carvings, mud volcanoes, and unique geological formations. Don't forget to take a guided tour to learn about the history and significance of the petroglyphs.

Climb Maiden Tower: Ascend the Maiden Tower for panoramic views of Baku and the Caspian Sea. Inside, you'll find a museum that sheds light on the tower's history.

Visit Heydar Mosque: Admire the grandeur of Heydar Mosque, one of the largest mosques in the Caucasus. Its stunning architecture and peaceful atmosphere make it worth a visit.

Explore Modern Shopping Districts: Stroll along Nizami Street and Fountain Square for shopping, dining, and entertainment. Explore modern malls like Ganjlik Mall and Park Bulvar.

Take a Day Trip to Nearby Attractions: Consider day trips to places like Sheki, Gabala, Guba, and Quba to explore the beautiful countryside, historical sites, and outdoor activities.

Experience Azeri Tea Culture: Visit a traditional teahouse and experience Azerbaijani tea culture. Try aromatic teas served with jam and local pastries.

Participate in Local Festivals: Check the event calendar for local festivals and celebrations. Novruz Bayram, Baku Jazz Festival, and Baku International Film Festival are some notable events.

Relax in Baku Parks: Spend time in the city's parks, such as Khan Shushinski Park and Khagani Park, to relax and enjoy green spaces.

These activities will help you immerse yourself in the culture, history, and vibrant atmosphere of Baku. Whether you're a history buff, an art enthusiast, or an outdoor adventurer, Baku has something to offer for every traveler.

how is the nightlife in Baku and what are the best nightlife spots

Baku has a vibrant nightlife scene that offers a mix of entertainment options, from trendy clubs and bars to live music venues and cultural performances. Here's an overview of the nightlife in Baku and some of the best nightlife spots to explore:

Nightlife in Baku:

Nightclub Scene: Baku boasts a thriving nightclub scene, with many venues open until the early hours of the morning. Electronic dance music (EDM) is particularly popular, and you can find top DJs performing regularly.

Live Music: Baku has a growing live music scene with venues featuring local and international bands, jazz ensembles, and traditional Azerbaijani music performances.

Cocktail Bars: The city has a growing number of cocktail bars that offer creative and well-crafted drinks. These bars often have stylish and sophisticated atmospheres.

Late-Night Cafes: Many cafes in Baku stay open late into the night, offering a relaxed atmosphere for those who prefer a quieter evening.

Casinos: Baku has several casinos if you enjoy trying your luck with games of chance.

Best Nightlife Spots in Baku:

Opera Sky Lounge: This rooftop bar offers panoramic views of Baku and the Caspian Sea. It's a great place for cocktails and a relaxed atmosphere.

Pasifico: Known for its vibrant Latin American music and dance floor, Pasifico is a popular nightclub in Baku.

Room 101: A trendy club with a focus on electronic music, Room 101 often hosts international DJs and themed parties.

Buddha Bar Baku: This upscale venue offers a mix of Asian cuisine, cocktails, and a laid-back atmosphere. It's known for its beautiful interior design and music.

Le Chateau Music Bar: A popular spot for live music, Le Chateau hosts a variety of musical acts, including jazz, rock, and local bands.

Nizami Street: The bustling Nizami Street and Fountain Square are home to many bars, cafes, and restaurants with outdoor seating, making them great places for people-watching.

Cigar Lounges: If you enjoy cigars, Baku has a few cigar lounges like The Shakespeare Pub & Cigar Lounge where you can relax and unwind.

Opera Club: This high-energy nightclub is one of Baku's top spots for dancing to the latest hits and electronic beats.

Chinar: A popular spot for upscale dining and live music, Chinar offers a diverse range of Azerbaijani and international music.

Baku Jazz Center: If you're a jazz enthusiast, check out the Baku Jazz Center for live jazz performances by local and international artists.

PARK Baku: This outdoor rooftop lounge and restaurant offers stunning views of the city and a relaxed ambiance, making it a great choice for an evening out.

Cabaret Show at Hilton Baku: Enjoy a unique experience with a cabaret show at the Hilton Baku, featuring live performances, music, and entertainment.

Remember that the nightlife scene in Baku can be quite dynamic, and the popularity of venues may change over time. It's a good idea to check local event listings and ask locals or fellow travelers for the latest recommendations during your visit to ensure you have a memorable night out in Baku. Additionally, be aware of local regulations and dress codes for some venues.

what are the best hotels in Baku

Baku offers a range of excellent hotels to suit various budgets and preferences, from luxury five-star properties to boutique hotels and more affordable options. Here are some of the best hotels in Baku, known for their quality accommodations and amenities:

Luxury Hotels:

Four Seasons Hotel Baku: Located on the waterfront of the Caspian Sea, this luxurious hotel offers stunning views, exquisite dining options, and world-class amenities.

JW Marriott Absheron Baku: Situated in the city center, this five-star hotel boasts elegant rooms, multiple restaurants, a spa, and an outdoor pool.

Fairmont Baku Flame Towers: The iconic Flame Towers house this luxurious hotel with stylish rooms, top-notch dining, and panoramic views of Baku.

Hilton Baku: Conveniently located in the heart of the city, the Hilton Baku offers modern rooms, a rooftop bar with breathtaking views, and easy access to major attractions.

Boulevard Hotel Baku, Autograph Collection: This upscale hotel is set along the Baku Boulevard and offers elegant rooms, a rooftop pool, and multiple dining options.

Boutique and Mid-Range Hotels:

The Crown Hotel Baku: This boutique hotel in the Old City offers comfortable rooms with a blend of modern and traditional Azerbaijani design.

The Landmark Hotel Baku: Located in the city center, this hotel offers contemporary rooms, a spa, fitness center, and excellent dining options.

Teatro Boutique Hotel: A charming boutique hotel in the Old City, Teatro offers cozy rooms with unique decor and a friendly atmosphere.

Divan Express Baku: This mid-range hotel offers comfortable accommodations, a restaurant, and a convenient location for exploring the city.

Staybridge Suites Baku: Ideal for extended stays, this hotel offers suites with kitchenettes, a fitness center, and a complimentary breakfast.

Budget and Value Hotels:

Central Park Hotel Baku: A budget-friendly option in a central location, this hotel provides clean and comfortable rooms for travelers on a budget.

Azcot Hotel: This value hotel offers basic yet comfortable accommodations and is a short walk from Nizami Street, a popular shopping and dining area.

Irshad Hotel: Another affordable option in the city center, Irshad Hotel provides clean and simple rooms for budget-conscious travelers.

Rigs Hotel Baku: Located near Baku's railway station, Rigs Hotel offers budget accommodations with easy access to transportation.

Balion Hotel: Situated in the Old City, this budget hotel is an excellent choice for travelers seeking a central location and affordability.

These are just a few of the many hotels in Baku. When choosing a hotel, consider your budget, preferred location, and the amenities that matter most to you. It's advisable to book your accommodation in advance, especially during peak travel seasons, to secure the best rates and availability.

Baku safe for tourists

As of my last knowledge update in September 2021, Baku, the capital of Azerbaijan, is generally considered safe for tourists. Azerbaijan, in general, has a relatively low crime rate, and violent crimes against tourists are rare. However, like any major city, Baku has its share of petty crimes such as pickpocketing and scams, particularly in crowded areas and tourist hotspots.

Here are some safety tips to ensure a safe and enjoyable visit to Baku:

Stay Aware: Be vigilant and aware of your surroundings, especially in crowded places, public transportation, and markets.

Use Reputable Transportation: When using taxis, make sure to use reputable taxi services or ride-sharing apps like Uber or Bolt. Insist on using the meter or agree on a fare before starting your ride.

Secure Your Belongings: Keep your belongings, including passports, wallets, and smartphones, secure and be cautious of pickpockets in crowded areas.

Avoid Street Scams: Be cautious of street vendors or individuals who may approach you with offers that seem too good to be true. Scams can happen in tourist areas.

Respect Local Laws and Customs: Familiarize yourself with local laws and customs, and be respectful of the local culture and traditions.

Keep Valuables Safe: Use hotel safes or secure lockers to store valuables when not needed, and avoid displaying expensive jewelry or electronics in public.

Emergency Numbers: Know the local emergency numbers, including the police, and have a copy of your identification and travel documents in a safe place.

Health Precautions: Ensure you have adequate travel insurance and are aware of any health precautions or vaccinations you may need before your trip.

Check Travel Advisories: Before traveling, check the latest travel advisories and updates from your government or relevant authorities.

Language: While many people in Baku speak English and Russian, learning a few basic Azerbaijani phrases can be helpful in certain situations.

It's essential to stay informed about the current situation and any changes in safety conditions, as circumstances can evolve over time. Additionally, the political and security situation can change, so it's advisable to check for any updates from reliable sources before your trip.

Overall, with common-sense precautions and awareness, Baku is a safe destination for tourists. However, it's always a good idea to exercise caution and be mindful of your personal safety while exploring the city.

what can i see in Sheki

Sheki, a picturesque city located in the foothills of the Greater Caucasus Mountains in Azerbaijan, is known for its rich history, stunning architecture, and natural beauty. Here are some of the top attractions and things to see in Sheki:

Sheki Khan's Palace (Sheki Khansarai): This magnificent palace is one of Sheki's most famous landmarks. It was built in the 18th century as a summer residence for the Sheki Khans. The palace is renowned for its exquisite stained glass windows, intricate frescoes, and ornate interior decorations.

Sheki Fortress: The Sheki Fortress, also known as the Sheki Castle, offers panoramic views of the city and surrounding landscapes. The fortress dates back to the 15th century and provides insight into the region's historical defenses.

Sheki Caravanserai (Museum of Folk and Applied Arts): This 18th-century caravanserai has been converted into a museum showcasing Azerbaijani folk and applied arts. Explore displays of traditional carpets, ceramics, textiles, and other crafts.

Gelersen-Gerersen Fortress: Located atop a hill near Sheki, this ancient fortress provides not only historical significance but also beautiful views of the surrounding countryside.

Sheki History Museum: Learn about the history of Sheki and the surrounding region through exhibits and artifacts at the Sheki History Museum.

Sheki Bazaar: Immerse yourself in the local culture by visiting the Sheki Bazaar. Here, you can sample fresh produce, spices, sweets, and traditional Azerbaijani snacks.

Sheki Albanian Church (Kish Church): Explore one of the oldest Christian churches in the Caucasus region. The Kish Church dates back to the 1st century and provides insights into the history of Christianity in Azerbaijan.

Sheki National Park: If you're an outdoor enthusiast, consider taking a hike or nature walk in Sheki National Park. The park offers pristine landscapes, lush forests, and opportunities for birdwatching and wildlife observation.

Sheki Silk Factory: Learn about the traditional silk production process at the Sheki Silk Factory, which is known for producing high-quality Azerbaijani silk.

Sheki Central Park: Enjoy a leisurely walk in Sheki Central Park, a green space in the city where you can relax and take in the peaceful atmosphere.

Gakh District: If you have extra time, consider a day trip to the nearby Gakh District, known for its stunning natural scenery, including waterfalls, rivers, and lush forests.

Azerbaijani Cuisine: Savor local Azerbaijani dishes in Sheki, including Sheki plov, pakhlava (a sweet pastry), and other regional specialties.

Sheki's charm lies in its well-preserved historical sites, beautiful landscapes, and the warmth of its people. Whether you're interested in history, culture, or natural beauty, you'll find plenty to see and do in this enchanting Azerbaijani city.

what are the best foods from Sheki

Sheki, a city in Azerbaijan known for its rich culinary traditions, offers a variety of delicious dishes that are unique to the region. When visiting Sheki, be sure to try these local specialties:

Sheki Plov (Sheki Pilaf): Sheki is famous for its version of Azerbaijani plov, which includes saffron-infused rice cooked with chestnuts, dried fruits, and aromatic spices. It's often served with pieces of lamb or beef.

Sheki Halva: Sheki halva is a sweet treat made from crushed walnuts and sugar syrup. It has a rich, nutty flavor and is often served in small squares or as a spread.

Piti: Piti is a traditional Azerbaijani stew made with lamb, chickpeas, potatoes, and aromatic spices. It's slow-cooked in individual clay pots and often enjoyed with bread.

Balish: Balish is a type of flatbread unique to Sheki. It's thin and crispy, with a delicious sesame seed topping. You can find it in local bakeries and enjoy it with tea.

Sheki Gurama: Gurama are small, deep-fried pastries stuffed with minced lamb, onions, and spices. They are a popular snack and can be found in Sheki's markets and bakeries.

Sheki Govurma: Govurma is a dish made from thinly sliced meat (usually lamb) marinated in herbs and spices, then slow-cooked until tender. It's often served with rice and vegetables.

Sheki Sudlu Piti: Sudlu Piti is a sweet version of the traditional piti. Instead of savory ingredients, it includes sugar, nuts, dried fruits, and spices, creating a delightful dessert.

Achma: Achma is a savory layered pastry filled with cheese and butter. It's a rich and indulgent dish that's perfect for breakfast or as a snack.

Sheki Kebabs: Like the rest of Azerbaijan, Sheki offers delicious kebabs made from marinated lamb, beef, or chicken. They are grilled to perfection and served with vegetables and bread.

Sheki Jengyal Bread: Jengyal is a type of Azerbaijani bread, but in Sheki, it has a unique twist. It's often baked in an oval shape and sprinkled with sesame seeds for added flavor.

Goy Gol Lake Fish: If you're near Goy Gol Lake in the Sheki region, don't miss the opportunity to enjoy fresh-caught fish prepared in various styles, such as grilled or fried.

Sheki Chai (Tea): Azerbaijani tea culture is an essential part of Sheki's culinary experience. Enjoy a cup of strong black tea served in small glasses, often accompanied by local sweets.

These dishes reflect the rich culinary heritage of Sheki, and trying them is an integral part of experiencing the region's culture and flavors. Don't forget to explore local restaurants, cafes, and markets to sample these delicious Sheki specialties during your visit.

what are the best restaurants in Sheki

Sheki, a charming city in Azerbaijan, offers a variety of dining options where you can savor traditional Azerbaijani and local Sheki cuisine. Here are some of the best restaurants and dining spots in Sheki:

Caravanserai Sheki: This restaurant is located in a beautifully restored caravanserai, offering a unique and atmospheric dining experience. It specializes in traditional Azerbaijani dishes, including plov, kebabs, and local sweets.

Il Bagatino: Il Bagatino is a European-style restaurant with a lovely garden setting. It serves a mix of Azerbaijani and European cuisine, making it a great choice for those looking for variety.

Xan Baghi: This restaurant is known for its picturesque garden terrace and authentic Azerbaijani dishes. Try their delicious piti (traditional Azerbaijani stew) and other local specialties.

Makhlai: Makhlai offers a mix of Azerbaijani and international dishes in a modern setting. The menu includes kebabs, soups, and a variety of appetizers.

Sheki Cafe: Located in the Old City, Sheki Cafe is a cozy spot to enjoy traditional Sheki cuisine, including Sheki plov and Sheki halva. The atmosphere is welcoming and intimate.

Toprak Galery: This restaurant combines art and cuisine, offering a unique dining experience. It features Azerbaijani dishes and is known for its artistic decor.

Caucasian Mountains: Situated in a picturesque location near the city, this restaurant offers stunning views of the surrounding mountains and forests. Enjoy Azerbaijani and international dishes in a tranquil setting.

Sehirli Tandir: While primarily known for its tandoori dishes, Sehirli Tandir in Sheki offers a selection of flavorful Azerbaijani cuisine.

Almali Restaurant: Located in a garden setting, Almali Restaurant serves a variety of Azerbaijani and European dishes. The atmosphere is perfect for a relaxed meal.

Xocali Lava: This restaurant offers a range of Azerbaijani and local Sheki dishes in a cozy and welcoming environment.

Please note that while Sheki offers some excellent dining options, the restaurant scene may not be as diverse or upscale as in larger cities like Baku. However, these restaurants provide a taste of authentic Azerbaijani cuisine and Sheki specialties, making your visit to the city a memorable culinary experience. It's also advisable to check the opening hours and availability of these restaurants in advance, especially during the off-peak tourist season.

what are some lesser known travel spots in Sheki

Sheki, with its rich history and stunning natural surroundings, offers several lesser-known travel spots and hidden gems for those looking to explore beyond the popular attractions. Here are some hidden and lesser-known travel spots in Sheki:

Gelersen-Gerersen Fortress: Located near Sheki, this ancient fortress offers panoramic views of the city and the surrounding landscapes. It's a peaceful spot with fewer visitors compared to some of the more famous landmarks.

Yeddi Gozel Waterfall: A short drive from Sheki, the Yeddi Gozel (Seven Beauties) Waterfall is a hidden gem surrounded by lush greenery. It's a beautiful natural spot where you can relax and enjoy the serene atmosphere.

Lahij: While not in Sheki itself, the picturesque village of Lahij is not far away. Known for its copper craftsmanship, Lahij is a charming place to explore cobbled streets, visit artisan workshops, and purchase handmade copper items.

Sheki Ethnographic Museum (Sheki Etnoqrafik Muzeyi): This small museum offers insight into the traditional lifestyle and culture of the Sheki region. It's a lesser-visited attraction that provides a glimpse into the local heritage.

Maraza Village: Located in the Sheki region, Maraza is known for its beautiful landscapes, including lush forests and rivers. It's a great spot for nature enthusiasts and those looking for outdoor activities like hiking and picnicking.

Albanian Church Ruins: Explore the ruins of ancient Albanian churches scattered throughout the Sheki region. These historical sites offer a unique glimpse into the area's early Christian history.

Sheki Mountain Villages: Consider venturing into the surrounding mountain villages of Sheki to experience traditional rural life and hospitality. You'll find welcoming locals, historic architecture, and stunning views.

Sheki Crafts School: Visit the Sheki Crafts School to learn about traditional Azerbaijani crafts and watch local artisans at work. It's a lesser-known spot for cultural exploration.

Karvansaray Restaurant: Located near the Gelersen-Gerersen Fortress, this restaurant offers a unique dining experience in a historic caravanserai. Enjoy local cuisine in an authentic setting.

Sheki Horse Riding Club: For those interested in horseback riding, the Sheki Horse Riding Club offers guided rides through the picturesque landscapes surrounding Sheki.

Shishi Khudafarin Bridge: Located a bit further from Sheki, this historical bridge is known for its picturesque setting over the Khudafarin Reservoir. It's a less-traveled area where you can appreciate the natural beauty.

While Sheki has some well-known attractions like the Sheki Khan's Palace and Sheki Fortress, these lesser-known spots allow you to explore the hidden beauty and culture of the region at a more relaxed pace. Be sure to ask locals or your accommodation for more information and directions to these hidden gems during your visit.

what activities must i experince in Sheki

Sheki, with its rich history, stunning landscapes, and cultural heritage, offers a range of activities to make your visit memorable. Here are some must-experience activities in Sheki:

Explore Sheki Khan's Palace (Sheki Khansarai): Begin your visit by exploring the exquisite Sheki Khan's Palace, a masterpiece of Azerbaijani architecture. Admire the intricate stained glass windows, frescoes, and opulent interiors.

Visit Sheki Fortress: Climb to the top of Sheki Fortress to enjoy panoramic views of the city and surrounding countryside. Explore the ancient walls and learn about the history of the fortress.

Discover Sheki Caravanserai (Museum of Folk and Applied Arts): Explore the Caravanserai to gain insights into Azerbaijani folk and applied arts. Don't miss the opportunity to see traditional crafts and textiles.

Hike to Yeddi Gozel Waterfall: Take a short hike to Yeddi Gozel Waterfall, located in a lush forested area near Sheki. The seven-tiered waterfall is a beautiful natural spot for relaxation and photography.

Learn About Sheki Crafts: Visit local workshops and craft stores to learn about the traditional crafts of Sheki, including copper craftsmanship, silk production, and pottery.

Taste Sheki Cuisine: Sample local Sheki cuisine, including Sheki plov, Sheki halva, and other traditional dishes, at local restaurants and cafes.

Wander the Old City: Explore the charming streets and alleys of Sheki's Old City, which is home to historic buildings, traditional homes, and local markets.

Visit Lahij Village: Take a day trip to Lahij, a nearby village known for its copper craftsmanship. Explore the village's artisan workshops and shop for handcrafted copper items.

Enjoy Sheki Nature: Embrace the natural beauty of the Sheki region by taking hikes, picnicking in the countryside, or simply strolling through the lush landscapes.

Attend Local Festivals: Check the local event calendar for festivals and cultural events that may be happening during your visit. Sheki often hosts traditional music, dance, and art festivals.

Learn About Azerbaijani Tea Culture: Visit a traditional tea house in Sheki and experience Azerbaijani tea culture. Enjoy strong black tea served with local sweets and pastries.

Explore Ancient Albanian Churches: Discover the historical Albanian churches and Christian heritage in the Sheki region by visiting ancient church ruins.

Sheki Silk Factory Tour: Take a guided tour of the Sheki Silk Factory to learn about the traditional silk production process and purchase silk products.

Photograph Scenic Views: Capture the scenic beauty of Sheki and its surroundings with your camera. The city and its landscapes offer countless opportunities for stunning photographs.

Interact with Locals: Engage with the friendly locals, learn about their traditions, and perhaps join in on some cultural activities or conversations.

Sheki offers a blend of history, culture, nature, and cuisine, making it an ideal destination for a diverse range of experiences. Whether you're interested in architecture, outdoor adventures, or simply enjoying the local atmosphere, there's something for everyone to enjoy in this charming Azerbaijani city.

. how is the nightlife in Sheki and what are the best nightlife spots

Sheki is primarily known for its historical and cultural attractions, and its nightlife is relatively subdued compared to larger Azerbaijani cities like Baku. While Sheki may not have a bustling nightlife scene, there are still some places where you can unwind and enjoy the evening. Here's an overview of the nightlife in Sheki and a few places you can visit:

Hotel Bars and Restaurants: Many hotels in Sheki have on-site bars and restaurants where you can enjoy a quiet evening with drinks and dinner. Some hotels offer live music or traditional Azerbaijani performances on certain nights.

Local Cafes and Teahouses: Sheki has a number of local cafes and teahouses where you can relax and have a cup of tea or coffee in a laid-back atmosphere. These spots are great for conversations with locals and fellow travelers.

Evening Strolls: Take a leisurely evening stroll through the Old City or along the scenic streets of Sheki to soak in the ambiance of the city after dark. The historic architecture and quiet streets create a peaceful atmosphere.

Local Markets: Visit local markets in the evening to experience the vibrant local culture and sample street food and snacks. It's a great way to interact with locals and savor the flavors of Sheki.

Hotel Terraces: Some hotels in Sheki offer rooftop or terrace spaces with lovely views. These can be great spots to relax with a drink and enjoy the night sky.

Cafes Along Nizami Street: While not a bustling nightlife scene, Nizami Street is one of the main thoroughfares in Sheki, and you can find cafes and small restaurants where you can enjoy a meal or a drink.

Local Events: Check with your accommodation or local sources for any special events or cultural performances happening during your visit. Sheki occasionally hosts traditional music and dance performances.

It's important to note that Sheki is a relatively quiet and peaceful city, and its nightlife is not as active as in major urban centers. Nightlife activities tend to wind down early, and the focus is more on experiencing the city's history, culture, and natural beauty during the day. If you're looking for a lively nightlife scene, you may want to consider visiting larger cities like Baku, which offer a wider range of entertainment options.

what are the best hotels in Sheki

Sheki offers a range of hotels to suit different preferences and budgets, providing comfortable accommodations for travelers exploring the city and its surroundings. Here are some of the best hotels in Sheki:

Luxury Hotels:

Sheki Saray Hotel: This five-star hotel offers luxurious rooms and a range of amenities, including a spa, indoor pool, and multiple dining options. It's located in a serene area outside the city.

Sheki Palace Hotel: This upscale hotel features elegantly decorated rooms and a beautiful garden with outdoor seating. It's known for its warm hospitality and traditional Azerbaijani cuisine.

Boutique and Mid-Range Hotels:

Sheki Park Hotel: A comfortable mid-range option, Sheki Park Hotel offers modern amenities, a fitness center, and a lovely garden area. It's located near the city center.

Shahdag Hotel & Spa: This boutique-style hotel offers well-appointed rooms, a spa, and a restaurant serving both Azerbaijani and international cuisine. It's a short drive from the city center.

Budget and Value Hotels:

Marxal Resort & Spa: Located in a serene location with beautiful mountain views, Marxal Resort offers budget-friendly rooms, a spa, and a restaurant serving local and international dishes.

Sheki Hostel: If you're looking for budget-friendly accommodations, Sheki Hostel offers dormitory-style rooms and a friendly atmosphere for travelers on a tight budget.

Hotel Sheki (also known as Hotel Shaki): This comfortable hotel offers basic amenities and a convenient location near the city center, making it suitable for budget-conscious travelers.

Please note that hotel availability and quality can vary, so it's a good idea to book your accommodations in advance, especially during peak tourist seasons. Additionally, amenities and services may change, so it's advisable to read recent reviews and check with the hotel directly for the most up-to-date information.

what can i see in Gabala

ChatGPT

Gabala, a picturesque city in Azerbaijan's Gabala District, is known for its stunning natural landscapes, outdoor activities, and historical sites. Here are some of the top attractions and things to see in Gabala:

Gabala Shooting Club: Visit the Gabala Shooting Club to try your hand at shooting sports, including clay pigeon shooting and archery. It's a popular destination for outdoor enthusiasts.

Tufandag Mountain Resort: Located in the Greater Caucasus Mountains, Tufandag is a popular ski and snowboarding resort in winter. In the summer, it offers hiking and scenic cable car rides with breathtaking views.

Nohur Lake: Enjoy the serene beauty of Nohur Lake, a man-made reservoir surrounded by lush forests and mountains. You can rent paddleboats or simply relax by the lakeside.

Yeddi Gozel Waterfall: A short drive from Gabala, the Yeddi Gozel (Seven Beauties) Waterfall is a stunning natural attraction with multiple cascades. Hike through the forest to reach the waterfall.

Tufandag Summer-Winter Tourism Complex: This complex offers a variety of outdoor activities, including zip-lining, paintball, and horseback riding. It's a great place for families and adventure seekers.

Gabaland Amusement Park: Gabala boasts an amusement park with rides, games, and entertainment for all ages. It's a popular spot for families.

Gabala Archaeological Center: Explore the Gabala Archaeological Center, which features exhibits related to the region's history and archaeological discoveries.

Chukhur Gabala: Discover the ancient village of Chukhur Gabala, known for its historical architecture and a mosque dating back to the 19th century.

Tufan Forest Park: Take a leisurely stroll in Tufan Forest Park, which offers a tranquil setting for picnics and relaxation.

Gabala City Center: Explore the city center of Gabala, where you can find local shops, markets, and restaurants serving Azerbaijani and international cuisine.

Gabala Olympic Complex: This complex hosts various sports and recreational activities, including tennis, swimming, and fitness. It's a good place to stay active.

Gavaldash: Gavaldash, also known as the "Singing Rock," is a large rock formation that emits musical sounds when struck. It's a unique geological attraction near Gabala.

Visit Local Villages: Consider taking day trips to nearby villages to experience rural Azerbaijani life, interact with locals, and enjoy traditional Azerbaijani hospitality.

Azerbaijani Cuisine: Savor traditional Azerbaijani dishes at local restaurants and cafes in Gabala, including plov, kebabs, and local sweets.

Gabala offers a perfect blend of outdoor adventures, cultural experiences, and natural beauty. Whether you're an adventure seeker, nature lover, or history enthusiast, you'll find plenty to see and do in this beautiful region of Azerbaijan.

what are the best foods from Gabala

Gabala, like many regions in Azerbaijan, offers a variety of delicious dishes that showcase the country's rich culinary traditions. Here are some of the best foods you can try in Gabala:

Plov: Azerbaijani plov is a beloved national dish, and you'll find variations of it throughout Gabala. It typically consists of saffron-infused rice cooked with vegetables, herbs, and your choice of meat (usually lamb, chicken, or beef).

Lyavangi: Lyavangi is a local specialty often found in Gabala. It's a dish made from minced meat (usually lamb or beef) mixed with rice, herbs, and spices. The mixture is then wrapped in grape leaves and cooked until tender.

Kebabs: Gabala is known for its delicious kebabs, which are skewers of marinated and grilled meat, often served with lavash (flatbread) and garnishes like grilled vegetables and pomegranate.

Qutab: Qutab is a popular Azerbaijani dish, and you'll find it in Gabala as well. It consists of thin, stuffed pancakes filled with various fillings such as minced meat, greens, and pumpkin.

Dolma: Dolma is a dish made from stuffed vegetables like bell peppers, tomatoes, and eggplants. The stuffing typically includes a mixture of minced meat, rice, herbs, and spices.

Shah Pilaf: Shah Pilaf is a rich and flavorful rice dish prepared with meat (often lamb or chicken), dried fruits, nuts, and aromatic spices. It's a hearty and festive dish.

Azerbaijani Sweets: Gabala offers a variety of Azerbaijani sweets, including baklava (layers of flaky pastry filled with nuts and honey), pakhlava (a similar pastry with a different preparation), and shekerbura (sweet pastries filled with nuts and sugar).

Gabala Apples: Gabala is famous for its apples, known for their crispness and flavor. Don't miss the opportunity to try fresh, locally grown apples or apple-based products.

Balish: Balish is a type of crispy flatbread often enjoyed as a snack. It pairs well with cheese, honey, or local jams.

Azerbaijani Tea: Enjoy a cup of strong black tea, a staple of Azerbaijani culture. It's often served with local sweets and pastries for a complete tea experience.

Local Dairy Products: Try Azerbaijani dairy products like yogurt (soghurt), ayran (a yogurt-based drink), and various types of local cheese.

Nuts and Dried Fruits: Azerbaijan is known for its high-quality nuts and dried fruits. Look for local varieties of nuts like hazelnuts and walnuts, as well as dried fruits like apricots and figs.

When visiting Gabala, be sure to sample these local dishes and explore the regional flavors of Azerbaijani cuisine. You'll find that the combination of fresh ingredients, aromatic spices, and traditional cooking techniques results in delicious and memorable meals.

. what are the best restaurants in Gabala

Gabala, a popular tourist destination in Azerbaijan, offers a variety of dining options, from traditional Azerbaijani cuisine to international dishes. While the dining scene in Gabala is not as extensive as in larger cities, there are several restaurants that provide enjoyable dining experiences. Here are some of the best restaurants in Gabala:

Qala Restaurant: Qala Restaurant is known for its traditional Azerbaijani cuisine, including plov, kebabs, and dolma. It has a warm and inviting atmosphere with outdoor seating options.

Gabala City Cafe & Restaurant: This restaurant offers a mix of Azerbaijani and international dishes, making it a good choice for those seeking variety. It has a pleasant setting with indoor and outdoor seating.

Qubek Restaurant: Qubek Restaurant is known for its flavorful Azerbaijani dishes and grilled meats. The restaurant often features live music, creating a lively atmosphere.

Karvansaray Restaurant: Located within the Gabala Shooting Club, this restaurant offers a unique dining experience in a historical setting. Enjoy a mix of Azerbaijani and international cuisine.

Vilaggio Italiano Gabala: If you're in the mood for Italian cuisine, Vilaggio Italiano offers a selection of Italian dishes, including pasta, pizza, and seafood, in a cozy atmosphere.

Azerbaijani Tea House: For a traditional Azerbaijani tea experience, visit one of the local tea houses in Gabala. Enjoy strong black tea served with local sweets and pastries.

Fast Food and Street Vendors: Gabala also has a variety of fast food outlets and street vendors where you can grab quick bites, including shawarma, sandwiches, and local snacks.

Hotel Restaurants: Many hotels in Gabala have on-site restaurants that offer a range of Azerbaijani and international dishes. These restaurants often have pleasant settings and may feature live music on certain evenings.

Please note that restaurant offerings and quality can change over time, so it's advisable to check with local sources or your accommodation for the latest recommendations and reviews. Additionally, some restaurants may have seasonal hours of operation, so it's a good idea to confirm their availability before your visit, especially if you plan to dine late in the evening.

what are some lesser known travel spots in Gabala

While Gabala is a popular tourist destination in Azerbaijan known for its natural beauty and outdoor activities, there are also some lesser-known travel spots and hidden gems that can provide unique and off-the-beaten-path experiences. Here are a few lesser-known travel spots in Gabala:

Gabala Shooting Club: While it's known for its shooting sports and activities, the Gabala Shooting Club also offers picturesque natural surroundings. It's a great place to visit even if you're not interested in shooting sports. Enjoy a walk around the grounds and soak in the scenic views.

Gelersen-Gerersen Fortress: Located in the vicinity of Gabala, this historical fortress offers panoramic views of the surrounding landscape and is relatively less crowded than some of the more popular attractions in the area.

Nij Village: Nij is a small village near Gabala that offers an opportunity to experience rural Azerbaijani life. Stroll through the village, interact with locals, and learn about their traditions and way of life.

Gabala Archaeological Center: This center showcases the history and archaeological discoveries of the Gabala region. It's a lesser-visited attraction that provides insight into the area's past.

Bum Settlement: Bum is a picturesque settlement near Gabala known for its natural beauty. Explore the forests, rivers, and enjoy the tranquility of the area. It's an ideal spot for nature lovers and hikers.

Traditional Carpets and Crafts: Visit local artisans and workshops in Gabala to learn about traditional crafts such as carpet weaving and pottery. You can observe the craftsmanship and even try your hand at some of these traditional arts.

Nohur Lake and Waterfall: While Nohur Lake is relatively well-known, the nearby Nohur Waterfall is often overlooked. Take a short hike to discover this beautiful waterfall, surrounded by lush greenery.

Gavaldash (Singing Rock): Gavaldash is a unique geological formation in the Gabala region. The rock emits musical sounds when struck, creating a unique and unusual experience for visitors.

Local Bakeries and Sweet Shops: Explore local bakeries and sweet shops in Gabala to sample traditional Azerbaijani sweets and bread. You can often find unique local pastries and treats.

Hiking and Picnicking: Beyond the well-trodden trails, consider exploring lesser-known hiking routes and picnicking spots in the Gabala region. Local guides can help you discover hidden natural beauty.

When visiting these lesser-known travel spots in Gabala, it's a good idea to have a sense of adventure and a willingness to explore off the main tourist path. Additionally, inquire with locals or your accommodation for more information about these hidden gems and the best ways to access them during your stay.

what activities must i experince in Gabala

Gabala, with its stunning natural beauty and diverse attractions, offers a wide range of activities for travelers to enjoy. Whether you're an adventure seeker, nature lover, or cultural enthusiast, Gabala has something for everyone. Here are some must-experience activities in Gabala:

Skiing and Snowboarding: If you visit during the winter months, don't miss the opportunity to hit the slopes at Tufandag Mountain Resort, one of the leading ski resorts in Azerbaijan.

Hiking and Trekking: Explore the beautiful landscapes surrounding Gabala by taking scenic hikes and treks. Trails like the one to Yeddi Gozel Waterfall offer both nature and adventure.

Cable Car Rides: Take a cable car ride at Tufandag Mountain Resort for breathtaking views of the surrounding mountains and forests, or visit the Gabala Shooting Club for a unique cable car experience.

Water Activities: Enjoy water-based activities on Nohur Lake, such as paddle boating or simply relaxing by the water's edge.

Gabala Shooting Club: Try your hand at shooting sports like clay pigeon shooting and archery. It's a unique experience for both beginners and experienced shooters.

Gabala Amusement Park: Visit the Gabala Amusement Park for a fun-filled day of rides, games, and entertainment, making it a great option for families.

Quad Biking and Off-Roading: Explore the surrounding countryside on a quad bike or take an off-roading adventure to discover hidden trails and landscapes.

Paragliding: Experience the thrill of paragliding over the picturesque landscapes of Gabala. It's an exhilarating way to take in the stunning scenery.

Visit Tufandag Summer-Winter Tourism Complex: Enjoy activities like zip-lining, paintball, and horseback riding at this complex, which caters to visitors year-round.

Gabala Archaeological Center: Explore the Gabala Archaeological Center to learn about the region's history and archaeological discoveries. It's an informative and educational experience.

Gabala Olympic Complex: Stay active at the Gabala Olympic Complex, which offers a range of sports facilities, including tennis, swimming, and fitness.

Gabala City Center: Explore the city center of Gabala, where you can shop for souvenirs, sample local cuisine, and immerse yourself in the local culture.

Local Cultural Experiences: Engage with the friendly locals, participate in traditional tea ceremonies, and learn about Azerbaijani culture and hospitality.

Visit Nearby Villages: Take day trips to nearby villages to experience rural Azerbaijani life, interact with locals, and enjoy traditional Azerbaijani hospitality.

Gabala Nature: Simply unwind and relax amidst the natural beauty of Gabala. Picnicking, birdwatching, and enjoying the tranquil atmosphere are all worthwhile activities.

Gabala offers a perfect blend of outdoor adventures, cultural experiences, and natural beauty, making it an ideal destination for travelers seeking a diverse range of activities. Whether you prefer adrenaline-pumping adventures or peaceful moments in nature, you'll find plenty to do in this beautiful region of Azerbaijan.

how is the nightlife in Gabala and what are the best nightlife spots

Gabala is primarily known for its natural beauty, outdoor activities, and family-friendly attractions, so its nightlife scene is relatively quieter compared to larger cities. However, there are still some options for evening entertainment and relaxation. Here's an overview of the nightlife in Gabala and a few places you can visit:

Hotel Bars and Restaurants: Many hotels in Gabala have on-site bars and restaurants where you can enjoy a quiet evening with drinks and dinner. Some hotels offer live music or traditional Azerbaijani performances on certain nights.

Gabala Amusement Park: The Gabala Amusement Park is a popular spot for families during the day, but it also offers some evening entertainment. You can find carnival games, rides, and food stalls in the park.

Cafes and Tea Houses: Local cafes and tea houses in Gabala offer a relaxed atmosphere where you can enjoy a cup of tea, coffee, or soft drinks. They are excellent places to unwind and have conversations with friends or locals.

Night Strolls: Take an evening walk through the city center or along the river to enjoy the peaceful atmosphere and take in the city's beauty under the night sky.

Hotel Terraces: Some hotels in Gabala have rooftop or terrace spaces with lovely views. These can be great spots to relax with a drink and enjoy the night scenery.

Karaoke Bars: A few venues in Gabala offer karaoke nights where you can sing your favorite songs and have fun with friends.

Local Events: Check with your accommodation or local sources for any special events, live music performances, or cultural shows that may be happening during your visit.

Star Gazing: Due to its relatively low light pollution, Gabala offers excellent opportunities for star gazing. Bring a telescope or simply lie down and enjoy the night sky.

It's important to keep in mind that Gabala is a relatively quiet and peaceful city, and its nightlife options are not as extensive as in major urban centers. Evening activities tend to be more relaxed, and the focus is often on enjoying the natural beauty and tranquility of the surroundings. If you're seeking a lively nightlife scene with clubs and bars, you may want to consider visiting larger cities like Baku, where you'll find a broader range of entertainment options.

what are the best hotels in Gabala

Gabala offers a range of hotels and accommodations to suit various preferences and budgets, from luxury resorts to cozy guesthouses. Here are some of the best hotels in Gabala:

Luxury Hotels:

Tufandag Mountain Resort Hotel: Located at the Tufandag Mountain Resort, this luxury hotel offers comfortable rooms, spa facilities, and stunning mountain views. It's ideal for both winter and summer travelers.

Qafqaz Riverside Hotel: This upscale hotel boasts modern amenities, a spa, an indoor pool, and a beautiful riverside location. It's known for its high level of comfort and service.

Qafqaz Sport Hotel: Another luxurious option from the Qafqaz Hotels Group, this hotel offers comfortable rooms, wellness facilities, and easy access to sports activities.

Mid-Range Hotels:

Gabala Hotel: Gabala Hotel provides comfortable accommodations, a restaurant serving Azerbaijani and international cuisine, and a convenient location near the city center.

Rixos Quba Azerbaijan: Located in nearby Quba, the Rixos Quba offers a range of amenities, including a spa, golf course, and various dining options. It's a short drive from Gabala.

Boutique and Family-Friendly Hotels:

Qafqaz Resort Hotel: This family-friendly resort offers a variety of amenities, including a water park, kids' activities, and comfortable rooms. It's a popular choice for families.

Qafqaz Karvansaray Hotel: This boutique-style hotel combines comfort and local architecture. It features a traditional Azerbaijani atmosphere and hospitality.

Guest houses and Local Accommodations:

Local Guesthouses: For a more authentic experience, consider staying in a local guesthouse or family-run accommodation. These options offer a chance to interact with locals and experience Azerbaijani hospitality firsthand.

Please note that the availability and quality of accommodations can vary, so it's advisable to book your stay in advance, especially during peak tourist seasons. Additionally, amenities and services may change, so it's a good idea to read recent reviews and check with the hotel directly for the most up-to-date information.Welcome to the enchanting world of Azerbaijan, a country that seamlessly blends rich history, captivating culture, stunning landscapes, and modern allure. Nestled at the crossroads of Eastern Europe and Western Asia, Azerbaijan offers travelers a tapestry of experiences that range from exploring ancient archaeological sites to indulging in sumptuous cuisine, from lounging on picturesque Caspian Sea beaches to immersing yourself in vibrant city life.

This travel guide is your passport to discovering the diverse and fascinating facets of Azerbaijan. Whether you're an intrepid adventurer, a history enthusiast, a culinary connoisseur, or simply seeking a unique and memorable vacation, Azerbaijan has something extraordinary to offer. Join us on a journey through the country's vibrant cities, tranquil towns, and breathtaking natural wonders as we uncover the best attractions, foods, accommodations, and activities that this remarkable destination has to offer.

Let's embark on an unforgettable journey through the Land of Fire, where ancient traditions meet modern marvels, and where the warm hospitality of the Azerbaijani people awaits you.

what can i see in Ganja

Ganja, Azerbaijan's second-largest city, is known for its rich history, cultural heritage, and natural beauty. It offers a range of attractions and places to explore. Here are some of the top things to see and do in Ganja:

Nizami Mausoleum: Pay a visit to the Nizami Mausoleum, dedicated to the great Persian poet Nizami Ganjavi. It's an important cultural and historical site.

Ganja State History and Local Lore Museum: Explore the museum to learn about Ganja's history, culture, and archaeological finds, including artifacts dating back to ancient times.

Nizami Park: Relax in the picturesque Nizami Park, which features green spaces, fountains, and walking paths. It's a great place for a leisurely stroll or a picnic.

Javad Khan Street: Wander along Javad Khan Street, the main pedestrian thoroughfare in Ganja. It's lined with shops, cafes, and restaurants, making it an ideal spot for shopping and dining.

Imamzadeh Religious Complex: Visit the Imamzadeh Complex, a historical religious site with a beautiful mosque, tombs, and intricate tilework.

Goygol National Park: Take a day trip to Goygol National Park, which is a short drive from Ganja. Explore the stunning Goygol Lake, go hiking in the surrounding forests, and enjoy the natural beauty of the area.

Khan Baghi Park: Discover Khan Baghi Park, a peaceful green space with walking paths, flowers, and sculptures. It's a lovely place to relax and enjoy the outdoors.

Nizami Mausoleum Mosque: Adjacent to the Nizami Mausoleum, you'll find a beautiful mosque with an ornate interior. Take a moment to appreciate its architectural details and peaceful ambiance.

Ganja State Puppet Theatre: If you're traveling with children or have an interest in the arts, consider catching a performance at the Ganja State Puppet Theatre.

Ganja State Drama Theatre: Check the schedule for performances at the Ganja State Drama Theatre, which often stages plays, musicals, and cultural events.

Ganja Archaeological Site: Visit the Ganja Archaeological Site to explore the remains of ancient settlements and gain insight into the region's history.

Ganja History and Culture Reserve: This open-air museum features replicas of historic buildings and monuments, allowing you to step back in time and learn about Ganja's history.

Local Cuisine: Savor Azerbaijani and local Ganja cuisine at restaurants and cafes throughout the city. Don't miss the opportunity to try traditional dishes like plov, kebabs, and pakhlava.

Ganja Promenade: Enjoy a leisurely stroll along the Ganja Promenade, which runs along the banks of the Ganja River. It's a pleasant spot for a walk or to sit and relax.

Ganja offers a blend of history, culture, and natural beauty. Whether you're interested in exploring historical sites, enjoying the outdoors, or simply experiencing Azerbaijani hospitality, you'll find plenty to see and do in this charming city.

. what are the best foods from Ganja

Ganja, like other regions in Azerbaijan, offers a range of delicious dishes that showcase the country's diverse culinary traditions. Here are some of the best foods you can try in Ganja:

Plov: Azerbaijani plov is a must-try dish. It's made with saffron-infused rice, cooked with vegetables, herbs, and your choice of meat (often lamb, chicken, or beef). Ganja's version of plov has its own unique flavor.

Lyulya Kebab: These minced meat kebabs, typically made from ground lamb or beef mixed with spices and onions, are grilled to perfection and served with fresh herbs, onions, and lavash (flatbread).

Dolma: Dolma consists of stuffed vegetables such as bell peppers, tomatoes, and eggplants. The filling usually includes a mixture of minced meat, rice, herbs, and spices, all cooked to perfection.

Ganja Kebab: Ganja is known for its delicious kebabs, which are grilled skewers of marinated meat, often served with lavash and various accompaniments.

Badambura: This sweet pastry is a popular Azerbaijani dessert. It's a thin, folded pastry filled with a sweet mixture of ground nuts, sugar, and spices.

Qutab: Qutab is a beloved Azerbaijani dish. These thin, stuffed pancakes can be filled with a variety of ingredients such as minced meat, greens, and pumpkin.

Sheki Halva: Though Sheki is another Azerbaijani city, you might find Sheki Halva in Ganja. It's a sweet treat made from ground nuts and sugar, often served in small squares.

Ganja-style Chicken: A local specialty, this chicken dish is typically prepared with a flavorful tomato-based sauce, herbs, and spices. It's a comforting and hearty option.

Azerbaijani Tea: Enjoy a cup of strong black tea, an integral part of Azerbaijani culture. It's typically served in small glasses and often accompanied by local sweets and pastries.

Local Dairy Products: Try Azerbaijani dairy products like yogurt (soghurt), ayran (a yogurt-based drink), and various types of local cheese.

Fresh Fruits and Nuts: Ganja and its surrounding areas are known for producing high-quality fruits and nuts. Sample fresh fruits such as apples, pears, and cherries, as well as local nuts like hazelnuts and walnuts.

Bread: Azerbaijani bread, especially tandoor-baked varieties, is delicious and worth trying. It's often served warm and fresh.

When visiting Ganja, be sure to explore local restaurants and cafes to sample these traditional dishes. The combination of fresh ingredients, aromatic spices, and traditional cooking techniques results in a flavorful and memorable dining experience.

what are the best restaurants in Ganja

Ganja offers a variety of restaurants and eateries where you can enjoy Azerbaijani cuisine and local specialties. While the dining scene is not as extensive as in larger cities, there are some great options to explore. Here are some of the best restaurants in Ganja:

Khan Baghi Restaurant: This restaurant is known for its traditional Azerbaijani cuisine and offers a lovely garden setting. Try their plov, kebabs, and local specialties.

Goygol Restaurant: Located near Goygol Lake, this restaurant offers a scenic dining experience. Enjoy a meal with views of the lake and mountains. They serve both Azerbaijani and international dishes.

Asad Karvansaray Restaurant: Asad Karvansaray is a restaurant designed in a traditional Azerbaijani style. It's a popular spot for enjoying local dishes and experiencing Azerbaijani culture.

Cafe City: Cafe City is a casual dining option in Ganja, offering a mix of Azerbaijani and international cuisine. It's a good choice for a quick meal or coffee.

Karvan Restaurant: Karvan Restaurant is known for its barbecue dishes and grilled kebabs. It's a great place to savor the flavors of Azerbaijani grilled meats.

Mestizo Cafe & Restaurant: This cafe offers a variety of dishes, including Azerbaijani cuisine and international options. It's known for its cozy atmosphere.

Chayxana Restaurant: Visit Chayxana for a traditional Azerbaijani tea experience. Enjoy strong black tea served with local sweets and pastries in a relaxed setting.

Al-Amir Restaurant: Al-Amir offers a blend of Azerbaijani and Middle Eastern cuisine. Try their kebabs, rice dishes, and mezze.

Gilan Restaurant: Known for its seafood dishes, Gilan Restaurant is a good choice if you're looking for seafood options in Ganja.

Local Bakeries and Sweets Shops: Don't miss the chance to sample local baked goods and sweets from local bakeries and sweet shops throughout Ganja.

Please note that restaurant offerings and quality can change over time, so it's advisable to check with local sources or your accommodation for the latest recommendations and reviews. Additionally, some restaurants may have seasonal hours of operation, so it's a good idea to confirm their availability before your visit, especially if you plan to dine late in the evening.

what are some lesser known travel spots in Ganja

Ganja has a mix of popular attractions and lesser-known travel spots that offer unique experiences for visitors. Here are some lesser-known travel spots in Ganja:

Nizami Street: While not exactly lesser-known, Nizami Street is often less crowded compared to similar streets in larger cities. It's a great place for a leisurely stroll, shopping, and trying local snacks.

Ganja Railway Station: The historical Ganja Railway Station is an architectural gem that's worth a visit. It features an impressive façade and has been recently renovated.

Ganja Automobile Plant: Visit the Ganja Automobile Plant to see how vehicles are manufactured in Azerbaijan. It's an interesting industrial attraction and offers insights into the local economy.

Agricultural Market: Explore the local agricultural market in Ganja to get a glimpse of daily life. You can find fresh produce, local products, and a vibrant atmosphere.

Ganja State Puppet Theatre: While not exactly a hidden gem, the Ganja State Puppet Theatre is a delightful spot for families. Check if there are puppet shows or performances during your visit.

Bottle House: The Bottle House is a quirky and unique attraction in Ganja. It's a house constructed entirely from glass bottles and is an interesting example of recycling and creativity.

Ganja Philharmonic Hall: This architectural landmark is often overlooked by tourists. It's a beautiful building with a striking exterior design.

Ganja Hippodrome: If you're interested in horse racing and equestrian events, check out the Ganja Hippodrome. You may have the opportunity to watch local races.

Local Cafes and Teahouses: Explore local cafes and teahouses in Ganja to experience everyday life and enjoy Azerbaijani tea, coffee, and snacks in a relaxed setting.

Ganja Bazaar: While not entirely off the beaten path, the local bazaar in Ganja is less crowded than those in larger cities. You can shop for fresh produce, spices, and local products.

Sheki-Ganja Friendship Park: This park, dedicated to the friendship between Sheki and Ganja, offers green spaces, walking paths, and a peaceful atmosphere.

Ganja Spring: Visit the Ganja Spring, a natural spring where locals come to collect fresh spring water. It's a great place to interact with locals and witness a daily ritual.

These lesser-known spots in Ganja provide a glimpse into the city's local culture, history, and daily life. While they may not be major tourist attractions, they offer a more authentic and off-the-beaten-path experience for travelers interested in exploring beyond the usual landmarks.

what activities must i experince in Ganja

Ganja offers a variety of activities for visitors to experience, from exploring historical and cultural sites to enjoying the natural beauty of the region. Here are some must-experience activities in Ganja:

Visit Nizami Mausoleum: Pay homage to the great Persian poet Nizami Ganjavi at his mausoleum. The beautiful complex features intricate tilework and a tranquil garden.

Explore Nizami Park: Take a leisurely stroll through Nizami Park, located in the heart of Ganja. It's a popular spot for both locals and visitors to relax and enjoy the greenery.

Ganja State History and Local Lore Museum: Discover the history and culture of Ganja and the surrounding region through the exhibits and artifacts in this museum.

Goygol National Park: Take a day trip to Goygol National Park to explore the stunning Goygol Lake, surrounded by forests and hiking trails. It's a natural gem not far from Ganja.

Ganja State Drama Theatre: Check the schedule for performances at the Ganja State Drama Theatre, which often stages plays, musicals, and cultural events.

Javad Khan Street: Explore Javad Khan Street, Ganja's main pedestrian street. It's lined with shops, cafes, and restaurants, making it a great place to stroll, shop, and dine.

Ganja History and Culture Reserve: Visit this open-air museum to see replicas of historic buildings and monuments, providing insight into Ganja's past.

Ganja Promenade: Enjoy a leisurely walk along the Ganja Promenade, which runs along the Ganja River. It's a picturesque spot for a peaceful stroll.

Ganja Railway Station: Admire the architecture of the historic Ganja Railway Station, which has been recently renovated and is a notable landmark in the city.

Local Cuisine: Savor Azerbaijani and local Ganja cuisine at restaurants and cafes throughout the city. Don't miss the opportunity to try traditional dishes like plov, kebabs, and pakhlava.

Ganja Spring: Visit the Ganja Spring, where locals collect fresh spring water. It's a great place to interact with locals and observe daily life.

Sheki-Ganja Friendship Park: Spend some time in this park, dedicated to the friendship between Sheki and Ganja. Enjoy the green spaces, walking paths, and a peaceful atmosphere.

Local Markets: Explore local markets and bazaars to immerse yourself in the daily life of Ganja. You can shop for fresh produce, spices, and local products.

Cafes and Teahouses: Experience Azerbaijani tea culture by visiting local cafes and teahouses, where you can enjoy strong black tea, coffee, and traditional snacks.

Ganja Automobile Plant: If you're interested in industry and technology, consider taking a tour of the Ganja Automobile Plant to see how vehicles are manufactured in Azerbaijan.

These activities offer a blend of cultural experiences, outdoor exploration, and opportunities to relax and enjoy the city's atmosphere. Ganja provides a unique perspective on Azerbaijani culture and history, making it a rewarding destination for travelers.

how is the nightlife in Ganja and what are the best nightlife spots

Ganja, while not known for its vibrant nightlife scene like some larger cities, still offers some options for evening entertainment. The nightlife in Ganja is relatively low-key and centers around dining, cafes, and a few bars. Here's an overview of the nightlife in Ganja and a few places you can visit:

Local Cafes and Restaurants: Many locals and visitors in Ganja spend their evenings at local cafes and restaurants. You can enjoy Azerbaijani cuisine, relax with friends, and soak in the ambiance. Some cafes may offer live music or cultural performances on occasion.

Teahouses: Azerbaijani teahouses are popular gathering places, and you can experience traditional tea culture in Ganja. Enjoy strong black tea served with local sweets and pastries while engaging in conversations with locals.

Javad Khan Street: While not a traditional nightlife district, Javad Khan Street is a popular pedestrian street lined with shops, cafes, and restaurants. It's a pleasant place for an evening stroll and dining.

Hotel Bars and Lounges: Some hotels in Ganja have bars and lounges where you can have a drink and unwind. Check with your accommodation to see if they offer such facilities.

Local Events and Performances: Keep an eye out for local events, cultural performances, and music concerts happening in Ganja during your visit. These can provide enjoyable evening entertainment.

Social Clubs: Ganja has a few social clubs where you can meet locals and fellow travelers, socialize, and enjoy drinks in a relaxed atmosphere.

Nighttime Walks: Taking a nighttime walk along the Ganja Promenade or through Nizami Park can be a serene and peaceful way to enjoy the city's atmosphere after dark.

Karaoke Bars: Some venues in Ganja offer karaoke nights, allowing you to showcase your singing talent or simply enjoy the performances of others.

Local Markets: Visit local markets and bazaars during the evening hours to experience a different side of daily life in Ganja. It can be an interesting and authentic nighttime activity.

It's important to note that Ganja's nightlife is quieter compared to larger cities, and most establishments close relatively early in the evening. The focus is often on relaxation and enjoying the local culture and cuisine. If you're seeking a more vibrant nightlife scene with nightclubs and late-night entertainment, you may want to consider visiting larger cities like Baku. Ganja, however, provides a unique opportunity to immerse yourself in Azerbaijani culture and enjoy a laid-back evening.

what are the best hotels in Ganja

Ganja offers a range of hotels and accommodations to suit various preferences and budgets. Here are some of the best hotels in Ganja:

Luxury Hotels:

Ramada Plaza Ganja Hotel: This upscale hotel offers modern amenities, spacious rooms, and excellent service. It features a restaurant, fitness center, and conference facilities.

Karvansaray Hotel: Karvansaray Hotel is known for its comfortable rooms, traditional Azerbaijani architecture, and a cozy atmosphere. It's a popular choice for both business and leisure travelers.

Mid-Range Hotels:

Ganja Hotel: Ganja Hotel provides comfortable accommodations, a restaurant serving Azerbaijani and international cuisine, and a convenient location near the city center.

Javad Khan Hotel: Javad Khan Hotel offers comfortable rooms and a central location. It's known for its friendly staff and good value for money.

Budget and Guesthouse Options:

Ganja Hostel: If you're traveling on a budget, Ganja Hostel offers affordable dormitory-style accommodations with shared facilities. It's a good choice for backpackers and budget-conscious travelers.

Local Guesthouses: Consider staying in local guesthouses or homestays for a more authentic experience and a chance to interact with locals.

Please note that while these are some of the best-known hotels in Ganja, the availability and quality of accommodations can change over time, so it's advisable to book your stay in advance, especially during peak tourist seasons. Additionally, amenities and services may change, so it's a good idea to read recent reviews and check with the hotel directly for the most up-to-date information.

what can i see in Gobustan National Park

Gobustan National Park, also known as Gobustan Rock Art Cultural Landscape, is a UNESCO World Heritage Site located in Azerbaijan. This remarkable site is renowned for its ancient rock carvings, mud volcanoes, and unique geological formations. Here's what you can see and explore in Gobustan National Park:

Rock Carvings (Petroglyphs): The most famous attraction in Gobustan is its extensive collection of rock carvings, which date back to between 5,000 and 40,000 years ago. These petroglyphs provide valuable insights into the prehistoric cultures of the region. The carvings depict scenes of hunting, dancing, rituals, animals, and daily life.

Gaval Dash: The Gaval Dash, or "singing rock," is a large, flat stone that produces musical sounds when struck. Local legends say that it was used as a musical instrument during ancient ceremonies.

Mud Volcanoes: Gobustan is home to numerous mud volcanoes, some of which are active. The landscape is dotted with these unique geological features, which create a surreal, otherworldly atmosphere.

Gaval Dash Museum: The Gobustan Museum near the entrance to the park offers insights into the history, archaeology, and geology of the area. It's a good starting point for understanding the significance of Gobustan's cultural and natural heritage.

Bibi-Heybat Mosque: Located near Gobustan, the Bibi-Heybat Mosque is a beautifully designed mosque that offers scenic views of the Caspian Sea. It's a notable religious and architectural site in the area.

Ancient Settlements: While exploring Gobustan, you may come across the remains of ancient settlements and archaeological sites. These provide further evidence of human habitation in the area throughout history.

Mud Bathing: Some visitors choose to take mud baths in the therapeutic mud pools near the mud volcanoes. It's believed to have healing properties for the skin.

Scenic Views: Gobustan offers stunning panoramic views of the Caspian Sea, the surrounding desert landscape, and the nearby mountains. Be sure to take in the breathtaking vistas during your visit.

When visiting Gobustan National Park, it's a good idea to hire a local guide who can provide insights into the history, culture, and significance of the petroglyphs and the park's natural wonders. The site is both culturally and scientifically significant, and exploring it with a knowledgeable guide can enhance your understanding and appreciation of this unique World Heritage Site.

what are the best foods from Gobustan National Park

Gobustan National Park is not known for specific regional cuisine since it is primarily a historical and natural attraction. However, when visiting the area, you can enjoy Azerbaijani cuisine, which includes a wide range of delicious dishes. Here are some of the best foods you can try while visiting Gobustan and Azerbaijan:

Plov: Azerbaijani plov is a must-try dish. It features saffron-infused rice cooked with vegetables, herbs, and a choice of meat (often lamb, chicken, or beef). It's a staple of Azerbaijani cuisine.

Kebabs: Azerbaijani kebabs, known as "shashlik," are marinated and skewered pieces of meat (often lamb or beef) cooked over an open flame. They are often served with lavash (flatbread) and fresh herbs.

Dolma: Dolma consists of stuffed vegetables, typically bell peppers, tomatoes, and eggplants. The filling is a mixture of minced meat, rice, herbs, and spices.

Badambura: This sweet pastry is a popular Azerbaijani dessert. It's made with a thin, folded pastry filled with a sweet mixture of ground nuts, sugar, and spices.

Qutab: Qutab is a beloved Azerbaijani dish. These thin, stuffed pancakes can be filled with various ingredients, including minced meat, greens, and pumpkin.

Pakhlava: Azerbaijani pakhlava is a sweet pastry made from layers of dough, nuts, and sugar. It's often enjoyed during special occasions and celebrations.

Azerbaijani Tea: Enjoy strong black tea, a fundamental part of Azerbaijani culture. It's typically served in small glasses and often accompanied by local sweets and pastries.

Local Dairy Products: Sample Azerbaijani dairy products like yogurt (soghurt), ayran (a yogurt-based drink), and various types of local cheese.

Fresh Fruits and Nuts: Azerbaijan is known for its high-quality fruits like apples, pears, cherries, and nuts such as hazelnuts and walnuts. Try these fresh and delicious offerings.

Bread: Azerbaijani bread, especially tandoor-baked varieties, is delicious and worth trying. It's often served warm and fresh.

While you may not find specific foods unique to Gobustan National Park itself, you can enjoy these Azerbaijani dishes at restaurants and cafes in nearby towns and cities. Azerbaijani cuisine is known for its rich flavors and use of fresh, local ingredients, making it a delightful culinary experience during your visit to Gobustan and the surrounding region.

what are the best restaurants inGobustan National Park

Gobustan National Park is primarily a natural and archaeological site with limited dining options directly within the park. However, you can find restaurants and cafes in nearby towns and cities where you can enjoy Azerbaijani cuisine before or after your visit to Gobustan. Here are some dining options in the region:

Bibi-Heybat Restaurant (Bibi-Heybat Mosque, near Gobustan): This restaurant offers a picturesque setting near the Caspian Sea and serves Azerbaijani and international cuisine. It's known for its seafood dishes and scenic views.

Gobustan Restaurant (Gobustan Village): Located close to the entrance of Gobustan National Park, this restaurant is a convenient option for visitors. It offers Azerbaijani dishes, including plov, kebabs, and more.

Restaurants in Baku: If you're traveling to Gobustan from Baku, you'll find a wide range of dining options in the capital city, including restaurants specializing in Azerbaijani cuisine, international restaurants, and cafes.

Local Cafes: Explore local cafes and teahouses in towns near Gobustan for a taste of Azerbaijani tea, coffee, and traditional snacks.

Please keep in mind that the dining options in the Gobustan area are more limited compared to larger cities like Baku. It's a good idea to plan your meals accordingly and check with local sources for the most up-to-date recommendations and dining options available during your visit to the region.

what are some lesser known travel spots in Gobustan National Park

Gobustan National Park itself is the main attraction in the area, known for its ancient rock carvings, mud volcanoes, and unique geological features. However, there are some lesser-known travel spots and activities you can explore in the vicinity of Gobustan National Park:

Bibi-Heybat Mosque: While not exactly lesser-known, the Bibi-Heybat Mosque is located near Gobustan and offers beautiful architectural and scenic views of the Caspian Sea. It's worth a visit if you appreciate religious and historical sites.

Salt Mountains: Some parts of the Gobustan region are characterized by salt flats and formations. You can take short hikes to explore these unique landscapes and witness the natural salt deposits.

Gobustan Archaeological Site: Apart from the well-known petroglyphs, there are other archaeological sites and remnants of ancient settlements in the Gobustan region. Exploring these lesser-known sites can provide additional insights into the area's history.

Rock Formations: Gobustan is home to various interesting rock formations aside from the petroglyphs. Take time to explore these geological features, including caves and unusual rock shapes.

Local Villages: Visit nearby villages like Gobustan and Gaval Dash to experience rural Azerbaijani life and interact with local communities. You can also explore local markets and get a taste of daily life.

Birdwatching: Gobustan National Park is a birdwatcher's paradise. The diverse habitats in the area attract a wide variety of bird species. If you're interested in birdwatching, bring binoculars and a field guide to identify the local avian residents.

Picnicking: Many visitors to Gobustan enjoy picnicking in the scenic surroundings. Pack a picnic lunch and relax in the park's natural settings.

Photography: Gobustan offers numerous opportunities for photography, whether it's capturing the ancient petroglyphs, the stark beauty of the landscape, or the geological features. It's a great place for photographers to explore.

Gala Archaeological and Ethnographic Museum: While not within Gobustan National Park itself, the Gala Museum is located nearby and showcases Azerbaijani history and culture. It's a fascinating place to learn about the region.

Gaval Dash Museum: Located near the entrance to Gobustan National Park, the Gaval Dash Museum provides insights into the history and significance of the Gaval Dash (singing rock) and its role in local traditions.

These lesser-known travel spots and activities can complement your visit to Gobustan National Park and offer a broader perspective on the region's culture, history, and natural beauty. Be sure to check local conditions, respect protected areas, and adhere to any guidelines or restrictions when exploring these sites.

what activities must i experince in Gobustan National Park

Gobustan National Park offers a unique blend of natural beauty, archaeological significance, and outdoor activities. To make the most of your visit, here are some activities you must experience in Gobustan National Park:

Explore the Petroglyphs: The primary reason for visiting Gobustan is to explore the ancient rock carvings, or petroglyphs, that date back thousands of years. Take your time to walk along the designated paths and admire the intricate carvings depicting scenes of hunting, dancing, rituals, and daily life.

Visit the Gaval Dash: See the Gaval Dash, or "singing rock," and learn about its historical and cultural significance. If permitted, you can try creating musical sounds by striking the rock.

Mud Volcano Tour: Take a tour to visit the mud volcanoes in the area. The landscape is dotted with these unique geological features, and witnessing the bubbling mud and volcanic activity is a memorable experience.

Hiking: Gobustan National Park offers hiking trails that allow you to explore its diverse landscapes, from rocky terrain to mud volcanoes. Wear comfortable footwear, bring water, and enjoy the natural beauty.

Picnicking: Pack a picnic lunch and enjoy a meal in the tranquil surroundings of the park. There are designated picnic areas where you can relax and take in the scenery.

Birdwatching: Gobustan is a birdwatcher's paradise, with various habitats attracting a wide range of bird species. Bring binoculars and a field guide to identify the local avian residents.

Photography: The park's ancient petroglyphs, rugged terrain, mud volcanoes, and scenic vistas provide excellent photography opportunities. Don't forget your camera or smartphone to capture the beauty of the area.

Museum Visits: Explore the Gobustan Museum near the entrance to the park to gain a deeper understanding of the history, archaeology, and geology of the region.

Geological Exploration: Aside from the petroglyphs, Gobustan features intriguing geological formations, including caves and unusual rock shapes. Take the time to explore these unique features.

Enjoy Sunset or Sunrise: The park's stark landscapes and ancient carvings take on a different charm during sunrise and sunset. Consider timing your visit to witness these breathtaking moments.

Guided Tours: Hiring a local guide can greatly enhance your experience by providing historical and cultural insights. Guides can also help you navigate the park and find hidden gems.

Learn About the Ancient History: Immerse yourself in the prehistoric history of the region and imagine what life was like for the people who created the petroglyphs.

Remember to respect the park's natural environment and archaeological sites by following designated paths and not touching or damaging the petroglyphs. It's also advisable to check the park's opening hours and any visitor regulations before your visit to ensure a smooth experience.

how is the nightlife in Gobustan National Park and what are the best nightlife spots

Gobustan National Park is primarily a protected natural and archaeological site, and it is not known for its nightlife or evening entertainment. Visitors typically come to Gobustan to explore its rock carvings, mud volcanoes, and geological features during the daytime. The park closes to the public in the evening to preserve its historical and environmental integrity.

If you're looking for nightlife or evening entertainment, you will need to travel to nearby towns and cities in the Gobustan region, such as Baku, for more options. Baku, the capital city of Azerbaijan, offers a vibrant nightlife scene with a variety of bars, clubs, restaurants, and cultural events.

In Baku, you can explore the following nightlife spots:

Nizami Street: This bustling pedestrian street in Baku is lined with cafes, restaurants, and shops. It's a popular place for an evening stroll, dining, and people-watching.

Boulevard and Caspian Sea Promenade: Baku's waterfront promenade along the Caspian Sea offers stunning views and a pleasant atmosphere. It's a great place for an evening walk.

Nightclubs: Baku has a range of nightclubs and bars that cater to different music preferences and atmospheres. Some of the popular ones include Enerji Club, Pasifico, and Opera Sky Lounge.

Restaurants and Cafes: Many restaurants in Baku offer evening dining experiences with live music, cultural performances, and a vibrant ambiance. Be sure to try Azerbaijani cuisine at local restaurants.

Cultural Performances: Check if there are cultural performances, music concerts, or theatrical shows happening at venues like the Heydar Aliyev Palace, Azerbaijan State Academic Opera and Ballet Theater, or the Azerbaijan State Philharmonic Hall.

Casinos: Baku has several casinos for those interested in gaming and entertainment.

Please keep in mind that the nightlife scene in Azerbaijan may differ from what you might find in larger cities in other countries. Additionally, opening hours and availability of nightlife spots can vary, so it's a good idea to check with local sources or your accommodation for up-to-date information and recommendations during your visit to the region.

what type of accomodation is available for tourists in Gobustan National Park

Gobustan National Park itself does not offer accommodations for tourists. The park is primarily a natural and archaeological site, and visitors typically stay in nearby towns or cities and make day trips to the park. The most common options for accommodation near Gobustan National Park are:

Baku: The capital city of Azerbaijan, Baku, is the largest urban center in the region and offers a wide range of accommodation options, including luxury hotels, mid-range hotels, guesthouses, hostels, and apartment rentals. Baku is approximately a 1.5- to 2-hour drive from Gobustan National Park.

Gobustan Village: This small village is the closest settlement to Gobustan National Park. While there are limited accommodation options, you can find guesthouses or simple lodgings in the village. Keep in mind that these options may offer basic amenities.

Other Nearby Towns: There are other towns in the Gobustan region, such as Bina and Garadaghly, where you may find guesthouses or budget-friendly lodgings. However, accommodations in these areas are generally limited in terms of amenities and services.

When planning your visit to Gobustan National Park, it's advisable to book your accommodation in advance, especially if you prefer specific types of lodging or if you're traveling during peak tourist seasons. Staying in Baku offers the most diverse range of accommodation options and allows you to explore other attractions in the region before or after your visit to the park.

what are the best beaches in Azerbaijan

ChatGPT

Azerbaijan has a coastline along the Caspian Sea, and while it may not be as famous for its beaches as some other coastal destinations, it still offers some beautiful beach areas. Here are some of the best beaches in Azerbaijan:

Bilgah Beach: Located just outside of Baku, Bilgah Beach is a popular destination for both locals and tourists. It features sandy shores, clean waters, and a variety of beach clubs, resorts, and water sports facilities.

Shikhov Beach: Shikhov Beach is another beach near Baku, known for its scenic beauty and the presence of several beach clubs and restaurants. It's a great place to relax and enjoy the Caspian Sea.

Nabran Beach: Located in the northern part of Azerbaijan along the Caspian Sea, Nabran is a resort area with several beautiful beaches. It's a popular destination for families and offers a range of accommodations.

Novkhani Beach: Novkhani Beach is a relatively quiet and less developed beach area near Baku. It's a good choice for those seeking a peaceful escape.

Sumgait Beach: Sumgait, a city near Baku, has a beach that is a favorite among locals. It's a great place to swim and enjoy the sea breeze.

Pirshagi Beach: Pirshagi Beach, located east of Baku, is known for its tranquil atmosphere and the opportunity to rent beachside cottages for a relaxing stay.

Ganja-Gazakh Region: While not on the Caspian Sea, the Ganja-Gazakh region in the west of Azerbaijan has several picturesque lakes, such as Maralgol and Goygol, where you can enjoy beautiful natural settings and swim.

Astara Beach: In the southern part of Azerbaijan near the border with Iran, Astara has a coastline along the Caspian Sea. The beaches in this area are known for their lush greenery and natural beauty.

Please note that the Caspian Sea is a closed body of water, so the beaches do not have tides like those on ocean coastlines. While the beaches in

Azerbaijan are generally safe for swimming, it's essential to observe safety guidelines, particularly if you plan to swim in less developed areas. Also, the availability of beach amenities and facilities may vary from one location to another, so it's a good idea to check in advance if you have specific preferences or requirements.

what other spots are there along the Azerbaijan coastline

Azerbaijan's coastline along the Caspian Sea offers a variety of spots and attractions, in addition to its beaches. Here are some other notable spots and destinations along the Azerbaijan coastline:

Baku: The capital city, Baku, is the largest and most vibrant coastal city. It offers a mix of modern and historic attractions, including the historic Old City (Icherisheher), Baku Boulevard, the Flame Towers, and numerous museums and cultural sites.

Baku Crystal Hall: This iconic building along the Baku waterfront is known for hosting major events, including concerts and sports competitions. It's an architectural landmark worth seeing.

Bibi-Heybat Mosque: Located near Baku, this beautiful mosque offers stunning views of the Caspian Sea and is an important religious and cultural site.

Baku Ferris Wheel: Also known as the Baku Eye, this Ferris wheel provides panoramic views of the city and the Caspian Sea.

Martyrs' Lane: This memorial site in Baku offers a place for reflection and pays tribute to those who lost their lives in the struggle for Azerbaijani independence.

Azerbaijan Carpet Museum: Located on the Baku waterfront, this museum is dedicated to Azerbaijani carpet art and culture.

Lenin Palace: This historic building in Baku has served various functions over the years, and it's an architectural landmark along the waterfront.

Port of Baku: The Port of Baku is a crucial hub for trade and transportation and provides an opportunity to see the bustling maritime activity along the Caspian Sea.

Shirvanshahs' Palace: Part of the UNESCO-listed historic center of Baku, this palace complex is a prime example of medieval Azerbaijani architecture and history.

Sumgait: This city north of Baku has its own coastline along the Caspian Sea and offers a quieter and more relaxed atmosphere compared to the capital.

Astara: Located in the southernmost part of Azerbaijan, Astara is a coastal town known for its lush greenery, botanical gardens, and the Astara River that flows into the Caspian Sea.

Lankaran: Further south along the coast, Lankaran is known for its mild climate, tea plantations, and beautiful beaches. It's a popular destination for nature enthusiasts.

Khachmaz: This coastal town in the northern part of Azerbaijan offers beaches, resorts, and access to the Guba-Khachmaz region, known for its natural beauty.

Caspian Sea Cruises: You can explore the Caspian Sea by taking boat tours or cruises from various coastal cities, offering opportunities for fishing, relaxation, and enjoying the sea breeze.

The Azerbaijan coastline along the Caspian Sea provides a diverse range of experiences, from cultural and historical exploration in Baku to relaxing beach getaways in coastal towns. It's a region with a rich mix of natural beauty and urban attractions.

what are the best shopping experiences in Azerbaijan

Azerbaijan offers a variety of shopping experiences, from traditional bazaars and markets to modern shopping malls. Here are some of the best shopping experiences in Azerbaijan:

Baku's Shopping Streets: Explore the bustling streets of Baku, such as Nizami Street (Torgovaya), Fountain Square, and Rasulzade Street, where you'll find a wide range of shops, boutiques, and brand-name stores offering clothing, jewelry, electronics, and more. These areas are known for their vibrant atmosphere and street-side cafes.

Baku's Grand Bazaar (Taza Bazaar): Located in the heart of Baku, this traditional bazaar is a great place to shop for fresh produce, spices, dried fruits, nuts, and local Azerbaijani products. It's an excellent spot to experience the local culture and pick up souvenirs.

Tea and Spice Markets: In Baku and other cities, you can find specialty markets dedicated to tea and spices. These markets offer a wide variety of teas, herbs, spices, and dried fruits. It's a great place to explore the rich flavors of Azerbaijani cuisine.

Carpets and Textiles: Azerbaijan is known for its beautiful handmade carpets and textiles. Visit carpet shops and boutiques to browse and purchase intricate Azerbaijani rugs and textiles, which make for excellent souvenirs.

Traditional Bazaars in Regions: When traveling outside of Baku, explore local bazaars and markets in towns and cities like Sheki, Ganja, Gabala, and Lankaran. These markets offer a glimpse into daily life in different regions of Azerbaijan and often have unique regional products.

Malls and Shopping Centers: Baku boasts several modern shopping malls, including Park Bulvar Mall, 28 Mall, and Ganjlik Mall, where you can shop for international brands, fashion, electronics, and more. These malls also offer dining and entertainment options.

Azerbaijani Souvenirs: Look for traditional Azerbaijani souvenirs such as local sweets (e.g., pakhlava and shekerbura), miniature carpets, traditional hats (papakha), and national musical instruments like tar and kamancha.

Antique and Vintage Shops: Explore antique and vintage shops in Baku, where you may find unique items like old Soviet memorabilia, traditional Azerbaijani crafts, and collectibles.

Art Galleries: Baku has numerous art galleries and studios where you can purchase contemporary Azerbaijani art, including paintings, sculptures, ceramics, and textiles.

Jewelry: Azerbaijan has a long history of jewelry making. Visit jewelry stores to admire and purchase handcrafted pieces made from precious metals and gemstones.

When shopping in Azerbaijan, it's a good idea to be prepared to haggle, especially in traditional markets and bazaars. While larger stores and malls have fixed prices, bargaining is a common practice in more traditional settings. Additionally, it's a good practice to check the authenticity and quality of items, especially when buying expensive items like carpets or jewelry.

what historical sites can i visit in Azerbaijan

Azerbaijan boasts a rich historical and cultural heritage, and there are many historical sites and landmarks to explore throughout the country. Here are some of the notable historical sites and attractions in Azerbaijan:

Baku Old City (Icherisheher): The historic heart of Baku, Icherisheher, is a UNESCO World Heritage Site. It features ancient city walls, narrow streets, historic buildings, and the iconic Maiden Tower. You can explore centuries-old architecture, museums, and art galleries within the Old City.

Gobustan National Park: Gobustan is renowned for its ancient rock carvings (petroglyphs) that date back thousands of years. It also features mud volcanoes and unique geological formations, providing a glimpse into prehistoric life in the region.

Ateshgah of Baku (Fire Temple): This Zoroastrian fire temple is located in Surakhani, just outside Baku. It's a fascinating site with religious and historical significance, featuring eternally burning natural gas fires.

Gala Archaeological and Ethnographic Museum: Situated near Baku, this open-air museum showcases Azerbaijani history, culture, and architecture. You can explore reconstructed ancient buildings and learn about traditional Azerbaijani life.

Sheki Khan's Palace: Located in Sheki, this stunning palace is known for its intricate interior decorations and stained glass windows. It's a masterpiece of Azerbaijani architecture and a UNESCO World Heritage Site.

Ateshgah of Surakhani (Fire Temple): Similar to the Baku Fire Temple, this temple in Surakhani is dedicated to the worship of fire and has a unique history that dates back centuries.

Mardakan Castle: This medieval fortress, located near Baku, offers panoramic views of the Caspian Sea. It's a well-preserved historical site that provides insight into the region's history.

Shamakhi Mosque: The Juma Mosque in Shamakhi is one of the oldest mosques in Azerbaijan, dating back to the 8th century. It's an architectural marvel with a rich history.

Lahij: This historic mountain village is known for its traditional coppersmithing craft. You can explore its winding streets, visit workshops, and purchase handcrafted copperware.

Ateshgah Temple in Surakhani: This religious site was originally a Hindu temple but was later used by Zoroastrians. It's an interesting blend of architectural styles and religious influences.

Nizami Mausoleum: Located in Ganja, this mausoleum honors Nizami Ganjavi, one of the greatest Persian poets of the Middle Ages.

Azerbaijan Carpet Museum: Situated on Baku's waterfront, this museum is dedicated to Azerbaijani carpet art and culture. It showcases a stunning collection of carpets and textiles.

Sheki Caravanserai: This historic caravanserai in Sheki once served as a resting place for travelers along the Silk Road. It features distinctive architecture and a courtyard.

These historical sites offer a glimpse into Azerbaijan's diverse history, ranging from ancient petroglyphs to medieval fortresses and architectural marvels. Exploring these sites will provide you with a deeper understanding of the country's cultural heritage.

. write a conclusion to this travel guide

In conclusion, Azerbaijan is a captivating and diverse destination that offers a wealth of experiences for travelers. From the modern allure of Baku to the ancient history of Gobustan and the natural beauty of its Caspian Sea coastline, Azerbaijan has something to offer every type of traveler.

In this travel guide, we've explored the must-visit cities and regions, from the bustling streets of Baku to the historic sites of Sheki, Gabala, Ganja, and beyond. We've delved into the rich cuisine of Azerbaijan, its vibrant culture, and the warm hospitality of its people.

Whether you're interested in exploring ancient petroglyphs, relaxing on beautiful beaches, savoring delicious Azerbaijani dishes, or immersing yourself in the country's history and culture, Azerbaijan has it all. As you plan your trip, remember to check for the latest travel information and any entry requirements, and consider seeking the assistance of local guides to enhance your experience.

Azerbaijan's unique blend of tradition and modernity, along with its stunning landscapes and historical treasures, make it a truly remarkable destination for travelers seeking a one-of-a-kind adventure. So, pack your bags, embark on your Azerbaijani journey, and prepare to be captivated by the beauty and charm of this captivating country.

## Discover Azerbaijan: A Traveler's Guide to the Land of Fire"

Description:

"Experience the magic of Azerbaijan with our comprehensive travel guide, 'Discover Azerbaijan: A Traveler's Guide to the Land of Fire.' From the dazzling streets of Baku to the ancient petroglyphs of Gobustan, this guide is your key to unlocking the treasures of this captivating country.

Uncover the secrets of Azerbaijani cuisine, explore historical landmarks, and venture into lesser-known travel spots. Whether you're planning a cultural adventure, an outdoor escape, or simply seeking the best of Azerbaijani hospitality, our guide provides you with all the information you need to make your journey memorable.

With detailed insights into the best cities, foods, accommodations, historical sites, and activities, 'Discover Azerbaijan' is your trusted companion for a truly immersive Azerbaijani experience. Get ready to discover the Land of Fire - a land of ancient wonders and modern delights."

Printed in Great Britain
by Amazon